GLOBAL FORTUNE

GLOBAL FORTUNE

Authored by

KDSUSHMA

PENMAN BOOKS
A BOOK PUBLISHING COMPANY

PENMAN BOOKS

Office No. 303, Kumar House Building,
D Block, Central Market, Opp PVR Cinema,
Prashant Vihar, Delhi 110085, India
Website: www.penmanbooks.com
Email: publish@penmanbooks.com

First Published by Penman Books 2019

Title: Global Fortune
Price: ₹499 | $ 14.99
ISBN: 978-93-89024-18-0

LIMITS OF LIABILITY/DISCLAIMER OF WARRANTY: The author and publisher of this book have used their best efforts in preparing this material. The author and publisher make no representation or warranties with respect to the accuracy, applicability or completeness of the contents. They disclaim any warranties (expressed or implied), or merchantability for any particular purpose. The author and publisher shall in no event be held liable for any loss or other damages, including but not limited to special, incidental, consequential, or other damages. The information presented in this publication is compiled from sources believed to be accurate, however, both the publisher and author assume no responsibility for errors or omissions. The information in this publication is not intended to replace or substitute professional advice. The strategies outlined in this book may not be suitable for every individual, and are not meant to provide individualized advice or recommendations.

The advice and strategies found within may not be suitable for every situation. This work is sold with the understanding that neither the author nor the publisher are held responsible for the results accrued from the advice in this book.

All disputes are subject to Delhi jurisdiction only.

“

Dream Big....

Plan It.....

Take Action.....

—KDSushma (Global Fortune)

”

Acknowledgment

This book is based on the international business, its rules, strategy and planning and how the business system works. This book has been developed through a series of lectures and its primary focus is on international business. I would like to thank Mr. Parag Muley, for your incomparable support throughout my journey of 10 years in international business and every reason for me being in this position. Much gratitude for your constant motivation and acceptance of my every recommendation.

I am also grateful to Mr. Upendra Lele and Mr. Vinayak Anikhindi as you had faith in me and gave me the opportunities and responsibilities to handle every situation responsibly. Your guidance and teachings have built me the skill of tackling all the ups and downs in business. My heartfelt gratitude to my mentors, guide Mr. Sarang Bhola and Mrs. Vrushali Shah.

I have learned a lot while discussing with people such as our Consulting Editor, Mr. Chidiebere Moses Ogbodo, and we appreciate your efforts and contributions throughout this journey. Also, I would like to thank all my students as because of you, I got an opportunity to explore every sector and it was always an interesting challenge you gave me wherever you had any hiccups in the business. Also, this book would not have been possible without the staff of GF mission India Pvt Ltd as they constantly put this book as a priority and provided me sufficient time, space and ambiance to write the book. I know many times you have put your work aside and gave your valuable time to gather resources for my book. I am indeed very grateful.

Finally, I would like to acknowledge my friends, my mother, my husband, and children - Kaushal and Dhruvi. You've always understood the priority of my book and without any complaint; you supported me with love and affection.

This book would not have been complete without my two heroes - Lord Ganesha and my Father who have been with me in every difficult situation. Thanks for filling my soul with love, joy, and confidence. I'll always like to interact and connect with you. Thanks for always be with me. Gratitude!!!

Introduction

Why Start Business

Do you know what motivates you the most or what scares you a lot? What is that thing that excites you or tries to draw you back?

If you can find out that you can lead a life of purpose and you can achieve your dreams easily and effectively.

However, many people have dreams, but they don't know what pushes them to see dreams or what stops them from achieving it.

I must say every person has to see dreams much bigger and bigger so that you can see the pictures of life you want to live.

You may have dreamed such as; I want to go on the world tour, I should have my bungalow, my luxury cars, and all the beautiful things in life. You have to remember that only imagination will not work; you have to think out the strategies that will enable you to achieve your goals.

Now let's consider the ways to reach your destination;

If you are employed, you may achieve the goal of travelling the world, but you may need to be very patient with your employer to pay you and also you have to save from your paycheque before you can embark on your journey. In so many cases, you may have to wait for 10-15 years, and you will not be able to leave your duty post for any personal trip. So, this limits your life fun and freedom of expression.

The above sounds strange?!!! So, this is the time to think differently and do something different. The question would be what you need to do to make a difference?

Answer: Why not think about Business?

Contents

CHAPTER *One*

Why Export Import Business?

Export is a very catchy word. While some people think it gives a high margin, the others are thinking it is very risky.

For you: What do you think... is it; Risky or Profit Making?

Export means to send goods from India to another country and Import means to bring products from other countries to India.

Why Export/Import

Why people go for Exporting

What do you think, give me five reasons why you or people want to start or thinking to start an Export business?

Response:

There are many reasons people are starting Export and Import Business. You have to identify them correctly.

Some of the reasons are listed below:

Market Access

Market access has been increased because of the presence of internet technologies. With internet development, you can do business where and whenever you want. The Internet is bridging the gap across various platforms, and it encourages organizational growth. Globalization is an excellent example of Market Access, and it is helping to bring people and businesses to each other through the strategies of technology.

FTA

Free Trade Agreement - The Government is signing an agreement between India and Other countries. FTA is helpful to waive the Import duty on the imported products weather in India and Other countries.

PTA

Preferential Trade Agreement - PTA is helpful to reduce the percentage of duty up to some extent or give a margin of preference on the imported product.

Both PTAs and FTAs are helpful to grow your business worldwide.

Demand/Growth

India is a land of opportunities. It is a place where your business can easily grow and expand across the globe. To start every business, you need to understand the Gap in the different Markets. Export allows you to find out Gap in the global market. The important thing about discovering this gap is that you will get to understand where there is a need to supply a particular product and satisfy the demand. That will grow not just your business but also yourself.

Extending Product Life Cycle

The Product Life cycle is a management concept that applies to every business, human being, and Products. It is used to define how businesses run through Generation to Generations and Country to countries.

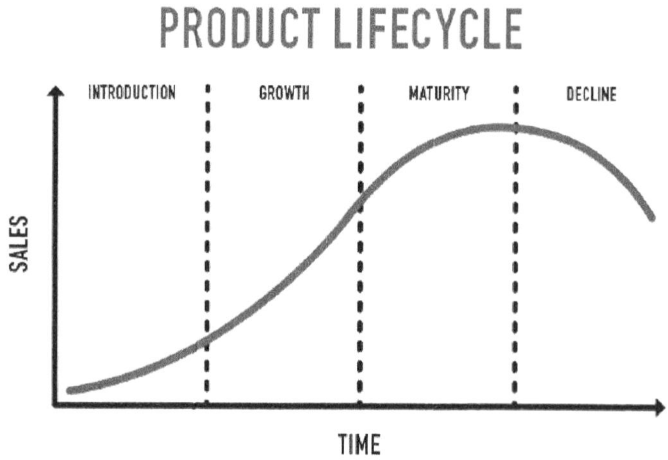

The businessman has to look into where the sales curve is going, identify the stage of the Product Life cycle and then act accordingly.

If you are at the maturity stage, then, you need to CHANGE something either, product, business plan, MARKET or yourself.

Change in the Market in this concern means you have to enter into **Export Business.**

Export Increases the Efficiency of Manufacturing

Export requires a product which is TOP, Medium and Low quality and fulfilling the criteria of the Importing countries, i.e. Quality parameters and standards of the Importing country. Manufacturing efficiency will be increased by accepting the quality standards of an Importing Country.

Respond strategically to foreign Competition

It helps you to improve your existing practices and product standards to beat the international competition, as your manufacturing efficiency is increased by enhancing and accepting the quality standards of importing countries.

Export from the Import

Many people in India are importing the goods for their End-use as Raw materials, Spare Parts and Prepare finished products from that; some people Import the goods to sell in Domestic Market.

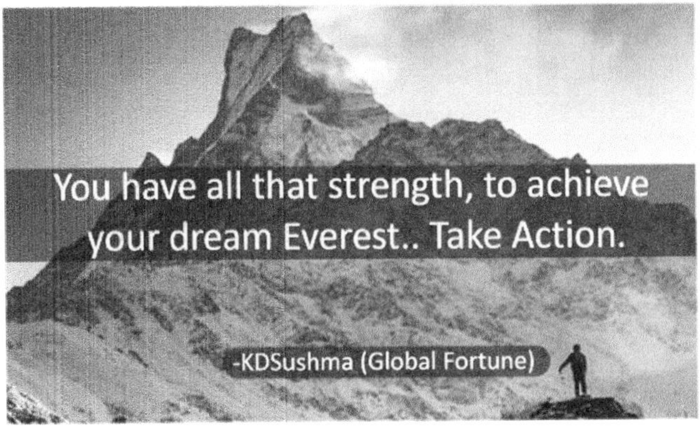

However, many people Import goods such as; waste and Scrap leather from Italy, process the products and prepare finished goods like Purse, Jackets, Shoes, Sacks, etc. for export and domestic sales.

CHAPTER *Two*

Scope of Export Business

Export has a vast scope. You can export anything from India and to the world.

Find out the Demand and Gap in the market.

Every country is depend on the other country and so the Export and Import is happening. For Example, India depends upon the Gulf for Crude Oil, Petrol, and Diesel, etc. And the Gulf depends upon India for Agriculture, Food and Spices.

Likewise, find out demand and supply in the market and start your business.

Sector wise scope for your ref. (*Source:* www.ibef.org)

Agriculture and Food Business

India is the largest supplier of Agriculture products, Food Products, and Spices. India has a basic resources such as: Fruits and Vegetables, Processed Food Products and Spices etc.

The Indian food and grocery market is the world's sixth largest, with retail contributing 70 per cent of the sales. The Indian food processing industry accounts for 32 per cent of the country's total food market, one of the largest industries in India and is ranked fifth in terms of production, consumption, export and expected growth.

India is the second largest fruit producer in the world. Production of horticulture crops is estimated at record 314.7 million tonnes (mt) in 2018-19 as per third advance estimates.

Total agricultural exports from India grew at a CAGR of 16.45 per cent over FY10-18 to reach US$ 38.21 billion in FY18. In FY2019 agriculture exports were US$ 38.54 billion. India is also the largest producer, consumer and exporter of spices and spice products. Spice exports from India reached US$ 3.1 billion in 2017-18. Tea exports from India reached a 36 year high of 240.68 million kgs in CY 2017 while coffee exports reached record 395,000 tonnes in 2017-18. (*Source:* www.ibef.org)

Engineering

A variety of engineering products manufactured in India. Comparative advantage vis-à-vis peers in terms of manufacturing costs, market knowledge, technology and creativity has been a driving force for engineering exports from India. In FY19, India's engineering export have crossed Rs 5,80,087 crore (US$ 83 billion). Engineering exports grew 6.32 per cent year-on-year to Rs 5,66,248.78 crore (US$ 81.02 billion) in FY19.

Textile

India is a hub of textile with large textile manufacturing units, and India is the largest supplier of Textile products.

Textile and apparel exports from India are expected to increase to US$ 82 billion by 2021. In FY19, India's textile and apparel exports increased 1.66 per cent to Rs 251,387 crore (US$ 35.96 billion) as compared to Rs 247,277 crore (US$ 35.381) in FY18. Manmade garments remain the largest contributor to total textile and apparel exports from India.

Animal, Meat, and Marine

India is the largest supplier of Marine, Animal, and Meat. India's exports of marine products to China has tripled and touched almost US$ 800 million, in the first nine months of 2019, as per the data released by China's customs authority recently. India's marine exports are expected to cross US$ 1 billion mark by the end of year 2019.

Services, Consultancy, and Teaching IT Services

Currently, India is a prominent supplier of IT services to the USA, UK, and Other Services.

Massive scope to IT services, Teaching, and Consultancy.

Education is in demand now. Many countries are under developing, and Literacy ratio is low, and they are demanding education. India is prominent in providing these services effectively and with high proficiency.

The question is: Are you ready to start your Export Import Business?

As we all know, there are many people who wish to start a business, but they are only having thoughts and leaving the right actions for another day.

Amongst the process of starting your business, the most important step is to learn about the business and everything related to it. If you would like to start the Export-Import business, then you need to undergo a series of necessary international trading training, such as provided at GF (Global Fortune) Mission India Pvt. Ltd. As learning basics of the business will give you confidence to move ahead easily. So learn either by self or from the Expert but Learning is essential to go ahead in the International Business.

Results will be achieved when there are series of action taken on daily basis. In all these, you need to start doing one or two things related to your business goals on a daily basis. So, TAKE ACTION

Learn and conquer the world.

– KDSushma (Global Fortune)

CHAPTER *Three*

Definition of Export and Import

It is quite evident that Export means to send goods from one country/ your country to another and Import means to bring a product from another country to your country. But this is in generic way. Sometimes there will be dispute between parties or any other stakeholders regarding to define it as a export or not. So Export Import has a defined definition.

For Example, The definition that was given to, "FOOD" by FDA is standardized, and you can fight every crisis in that regards using the same meaning. Considering the definition given to food by the FDA, the term Export and Import are also defined by the Customs:

Import

Bringing in to India from a place inside territorial waters of India which is 12 nautical miles into the sea from the coast of India'

Liability to pay import duty commences as soon as the goods entered 12 nautical miles into the sea from the coast of India.

Export

'Taking out of India to a place outside territorial waters of India which is 12 nautical miles into the sea from the coast of India".

(1 nautical miles = 1.852 kilometres)

CHAPTER *Four*

Procedures of Export and Import

Export and Import trade involve a level of involvements such as; Legal Procedures, Trade Partners, Stakeholders, and series of Documentations in the business.

In this part, we will learn now How Export and Import is done means which will include the procedures involved in the trade.

The practical sense of the business is explained in the diagram below:

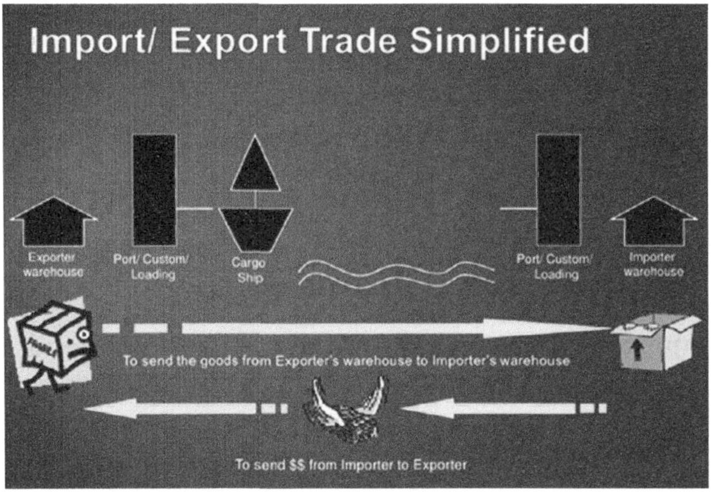

E.g. the image above can be defined as there is an Exporter Warehouse/ Factory in India and the Importers warehouse/factory is in Dubai.

Concerning the above, the most crucial part is that you have to know the Seaport, Airport and Road borders of both the Countries.

Assignment

Select at least 10 Countries that you wish to do business and find there corresponding Sea Port, Air Port and Road Borders.

____

____

____

Every Country has Seaport and or Airport and or Road borders.

Important Note

Exporter - A person or company that sends goods or services to another country for sale

Warehouse - Manufacturing place or Storage place of finished products, which are for Export / Import shipment.

Importer - A person or organization that brings goods or services into a country from abroad

Custom - Government authority handling the Export and Import clearances.

Vessel - A craft for travelling on water, now usually one larger than an ordinary rowboat; a ship or boat.

Port - An opening in the side of a ship for boarding or loading.

Custom Clearance - The documented permission to pass that a national customs authority grants to imported goods so that they can enter the country or to exported goods so that they can leave the country. The custom clearance is typically given to a shipping agent to prove that all applicable customs duties have been paid and the shipment has been approved.

Container - A large reusable receptacle that can accommodate smaller cartons or cases in a single shipment, designed for efficient handling of cargo.

CHA - A custom house agent is somebody entitled to act upon a company's behalf on actions involving the import and export of goods. Their such agents must be licensed under the Customs Act.

FF (Freight Forwarders) - Firm specializing in arranging storage and shipping of merchandise on behalf of its shippers.

Procedures - This includes general information on how Export and Import has been carried out.

Practically:

Exporter calls the vehicle in Factory/Farm, load the goods in that vehicle and dispatch the goods to the port (Any Port which includes either the Sea / Air in the respective region).

At the port, Goods are unloaded in the warehouse and again loaded in the Container.

The Agent (CHA / FF) organizes Custom Clearance activity and all the documentary procedures. Once goods have been cleared by the customs, it will move further and loaded on the vessel and as per the schedule.

When the Vessel Crosses the seller Border to the other side/region, then we can say Export has happened.

The Import agents await the vessel at the importers port. When the ship arrives at the destination port the Importers Agent (FF/CHA) will organize the customs clearance activity.

Customs will calculate the Charges, Duties, and taxes and after paying the same Importer will get the goods in hand, then it will move to to the Importer's warehouse or factory.

Certain documents are generated in these procedures which are required to clear the cargo from Exporting and Importing country.

This is the general procedure of the Export and Import of the goods.

In the exception of these significant activities, there are various other small activities, many stakeholders, and minor documentation in-between.

So, to study the Export and Import, you need to learn the procedures from Exporter warehouse to the Importers warehouse.

I hope you have got a rough idea about Export and Import and I know how you want to start your Export and Import Business.

CHAPTER *Five*

Starting Export-Import Business

Documentation Process

To start the Export and Import business, the documents required are listed below –

Practical Process and Documents

Form your Company

Obtain PAN

Open Current Account

Obtain an IEC (Import Export Code)

Register your IEC & AD code with custom (Sea & Air)

Register with GST

Get RCMC (Registration cum Membership Certificate)

Do your homework- Country Profiling

Form your Company

First, you have to set up or form a company. There are many ways to form or establish a company.

Proprietorship - a person who has the exclusive right or title to something; an owner, as of real property. And you are the only owner of a Business or a holder of the property. The property is owned and managed by only you.

Partnership - A legal relation existing between two or more persons contractually associated as joint principals in a business and having mutual rights and responsibilities

LLP - LLP stands for Limited Liability Partnership in which some or all partners (depending on the jurisdiction) have limited liabilities.

Private Limited - A type of company that offers limited liability or legal protection for its shareholders but that places certain restrictions on its ownership.

Public Limited - A company whose securities are traded on a stock exchange and can be bought and sold by anyone. Public companies are strictly regulated and are required by law to publish their complete and accurate financial position so that investors can determine the true worth of it's stock (shares). Also called publicly held company.

As per the above forms of company, it is paramount that you should know the necessary documents which are required to register your company, such as;

Note: The documents may differ as per the region/ country. Here we are focussing on the India market.

PAN Card

Every Individual and Business requires PAN Card, which stands for, Permanent Account Number (PAN). This is a code that acts as an identification for individuals, families, and corporates (Indian and Foreign as well), especially those who pay Income Tax and it is issued by the Indian Income Tax department.

You need to issue PAN according to the form of your company. If you are Proprietor, your own (Individual) pan card is applicable. If you are Partnership Firm, LLP or Private Limited or Public Limited Company, you need to obtain a PAN card for your Company.

Open Current Account

After the formation of your company and obtaining your PAN card, you need to open a Current Account with the bank of your choice.

Current Account - an account of credits, debits, receipts, and expenditures between two individuals or companies, usually providing for settlement at the end of specified accounting periods.

This resource is essential for your business.

Obtain an IEC (Import Export Code)

The first requirement before you start an import/ export business in India and everywhere across the globe is to obtain an IEC (Import Export Code).

An IEC is necessary for Import/Exportation of goods and services, and it is issued by various officials in countries such as DGFT in India.

It is crucial to note that document requirements vary as per the form of the company you want to operate.

Register Your IEC & AD code with custom

AD - Authorized Dealer Code.

It is the code given by the bank in which your company has a current account.

Get the AD code issued by a bank, IEC and other required documents together. Register your AD code and all other documents with customs, for port registration.

Register with GST

The Goods and Services Tax (GST) is a value-added tax levied on most goods and services in India. So, you need to register with your local tax body and get the GST no.

Get RCMC (Registration Cum Membership Certificate)

In India, we have different sectors like Agriculture, Marine, Engineering, Textile, Handicraft, Information Technology, etc and many more.

So, to promote export of that particular trade, the government has different Export Promotion Councils like APEDA, EEPC, Spice Board of India, Handicraft Export Promotion Council, etc.

The company needs to register with the respective Export promotion Council and get their membership (RCMC) certificate.

These are the basic documents required to start the Export and Import business. Apart from this, other documents or certificates will be required as per the product/stuffing/other factors.

Do Your Homework such as; Country Profiling

Once you are ready with all these documents, now the main important part is to study your Target Market. Do your homework of Country Profiling (Make a research on the Market), Study about the market, Economic Condition, Political Condition, Environmental conditions and all other aspects related to Market.

Without proper market study, it is not advisable to enter into the International market or start an international business.

CHAPTER *Six*

Types of Export

Export Types

There are many ways to start the Export business. You can Export and Import Goods and Services both.

Every business is done either directly or indirectly. In the Export business as well, we can do Direct Export and Indirect Export.

Direct Export - Selling directly to target customers in the market through the internet and regular trade visits, or by setting up a branch, office or company in the target country.

If you are exporting directly, you are called as a Manufacturer Exporter.

Manufacturer Exporter - This means a person who manufactures goods and exports or intends to export such goods.

Indirect Export - Selling to or through an intermediary.

If you are exporting indirectly, you are called as a Merchant Exporter.

Merchant Exporter - Means a person engaged in trading activity and exporting or intending to export goods. Merchant exporter procures the material from a manufacturer and exports in his firm's name.

Deemed Export

"Deemed Exports" refers to those transactions in which the goods supplied do not leave the country and the payment for such supplies is received either in Indian rupees or in free foreign exchange. So you are called as a Deemed Exporter.

Farmer is the best example of Deemed Exporter.

CHAPTER *Seven*

HS Code

The Harmonized Commodity Description and Coding System, also known as the Harmonized System (HS) of tariff nomenclature is an internationally standardized system of names and numbers to classify traded products.

The "Identification Number" of all products in the Custom procedure.

It is an internationally standardized system of names and numbers for classifying traded products

Example - The classification will change depending on whether the potatoes are fresh or frozen. Fresh potatoes are classified in position 0701.90, under the Header Potatoes, fresh or chilled, Subheader other, while frozen potatoes are classified in position 0710.10 under the Header Vegetables (uncooked or cooked by steaming or boiling in water), frozen, Subheader Potatoes.

It is important to find out the HS code of your product. You will get these details on DGFT or CBIC (Central Board of Indirect Taxes and Customs)

CHAPTER Eight

Incoterms

INCOTERMS

The Incoterms or International Commercial Terms are a series of pre-defined commercial terms published by the International Chamber of Commerce (ICC) relating to international commercial law.

The Incoterms rules have become an essential part of the daily language of trade. They have been incorporated in contracts for the sale of goods worldwide and provide rules and guidance to importers, exporters, lawyers, transporters, insurers and students of international trade.

Incoterms

It defines the roles, responsibilities, and risks of the Buyer and Seller, costs involved in the transactions and who will bear the cost up to the place of destination.

Incoterms are the base of Costing and delivery of the goods. It is used as per the Modes of transport, Product, Emergency, Country, etc....

RULES FOR ANY MODE OR MODES OF TRANSPORT

EXW Ex Works

"Ex Works" means that the seller delivers when it places the goods at the disposal of the buyer at the seller's premises or at another named place (i.e., works factory, warehouse, etc.).

The seller does not need to load the goods on any collecting vehicle, nor does it need to clear the goods for export, where such clearance is applicable.

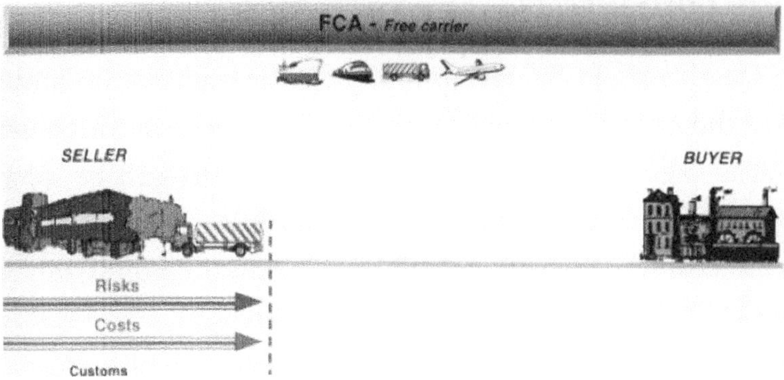

FCA Free Carrier

"Free Carrier" means that the seller delivers the goods to the carrier or another person nominated by the buyer at the seller's premises or another named place.

The parties are well advised to specify as clearly as possible the point within the named place of delivery, as the risk passes to the buyer at that point.

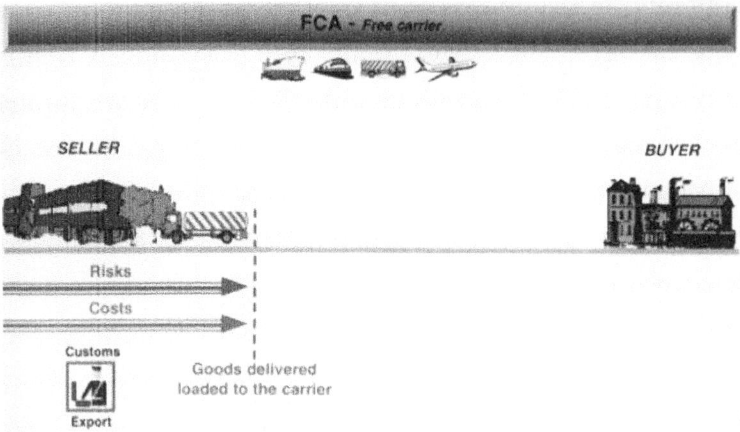

CPT Carriage Paid To

"Carriage Paid To" means that the seller delivers the goods to the carrier or another person nominated by the seller at an agreed place (if any such place is agreed between parties) and that the seller must contract for and pay the costs of carriage necessary to bring the goods to the named place of destination.

CIP Carriage And Insurance Paid To

"Carriage and Insurance Paid to" means that the seller delivers the goods to the carrier or another person nominated by the seller at an agreed place (if any such place is agreed between parties) and that the seller must contract for and pay the costs of carriage necessary to bring the goods to the named place of destination.

'The seller also contracts for insurance cover against the buyer's risk of loss of or damage to the goods during the carriage. The buyer should note that under CIP, the seller is required to obtain insurance only on minimum cover. Should the buyer wish to have more insurance protection, it will need either to agree as much expressly with the seller to make it's extra insurance arrangements."

DAT Delivered At Terminal

"Delivered at Terminal" means that the seller delivers when the goods, once unloaded from the arriving means of transport, are placed at the disposal of the buyer at a named terminal at the named port or place of destination. "Terminal" includes a place, whether covered or not, such as a quay, warehouse, container yard or road, rail or air cargo terminal.

The seller bears all risks involved in bringing the goods to and unloading them at the terminal at the named port or place of destination.

DAP Delivered At Place

"Delivered at Place" means that the seller delivers when the goods are placed at the disposal of the buyer on the arriving means of transport ready for unloading at the named place of destination.

The seller bears all risks involved in bringing the goods to the named place.

DDP Delivered Duty Paid

"Delivered Duty Paid" means that the seller delivers the goods when the goods are placed at the disposal of the buyer, cleared for import on the arriving means of transport ready for unloading at the named place of destination.

The seller bears all the costs and risks involved in bringing the goods to the place of destination and has an obligation to clear the goods not only for export but also for import, to pay any duty for both export and import and to carry out all customs formalities.

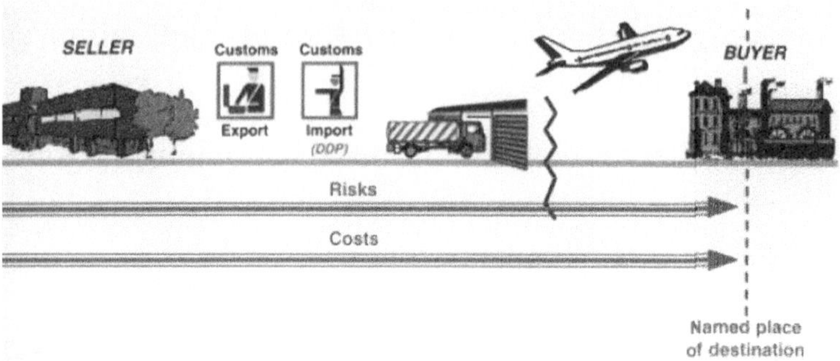

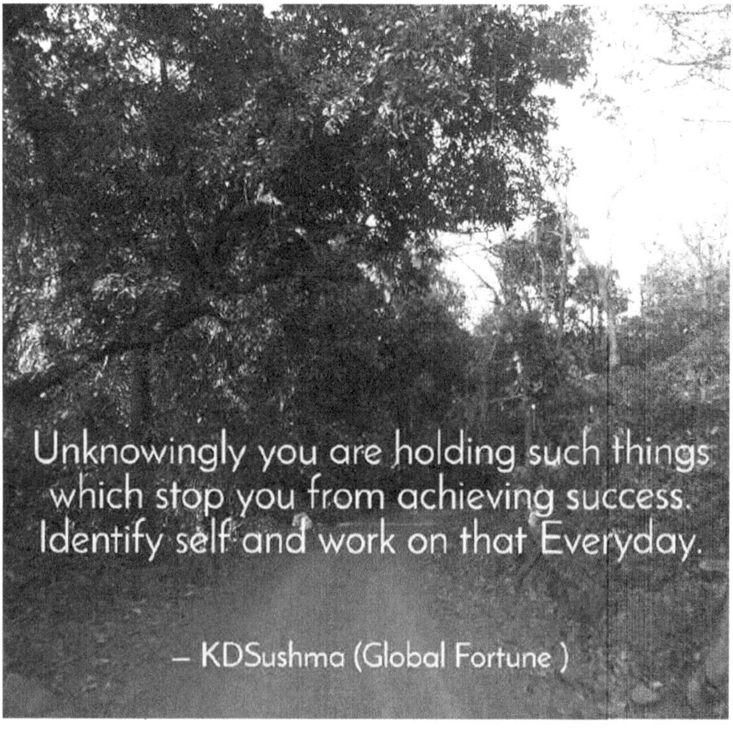

RULES FOR SEA AND INLAND WATERWAY TRANSPORT

FAS Free Alongside Ship

"Free Alongside Ship" means that the seller delivers when the goods are placed alongside the vessel (e.g., on a quay or a barge) nominated by the buyer at the named port of shipment.

The risk of loss of or damage to the goods passes when the goods are alongside the ship, and the buyer bears all costs from that moment onwards.

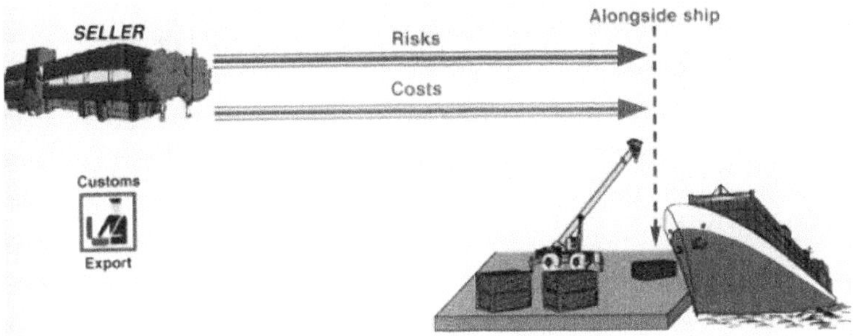

FOB Free On Board

"Free On Board" means that the seller delivers the goods on board the vessel nominated by the buyer at the named port of shipment or procures the goods already so delivered.

The risk of loss of or damage to the goods passes when the goods are on board the vessel, and the buyer bears all costs from that moment onwards.

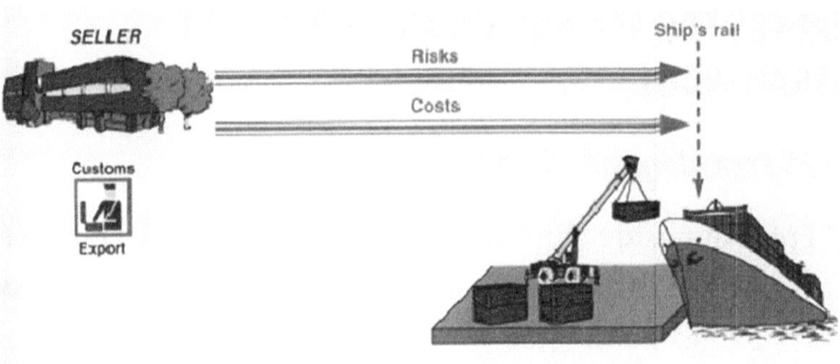

CFR Cost and Freight

"Cost and Freight" means that the seller delivers the goods on board the vessel or procures the goods already so provided. The risk of loss of or damage to the goods passes when the goods are on board the vessel.

The seller must contract for and pay the costs and freight necessary to bring the goods to the named port of destination.

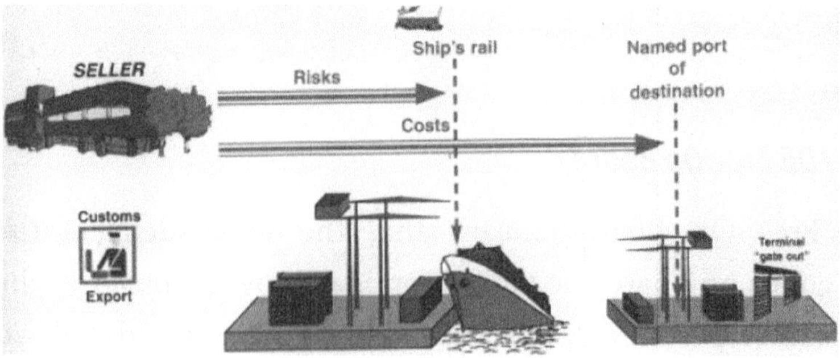

CIF Cost, Insurance and Freight

"Cost, Insurance and Freight" means that the seller delivers the goods on board the vessel or procures the goods already so delivered. The risk of loss of or damage to the goods passes when the goods are on the ship.

The seller must contract for and pay the costs and freight necessary to bring the goods to the named port of destination.

'The seller also contracts for insurance cover against the buyer's risk of loss of or damage to the goods during the carriage. The buyer should note that under CIF, the seller is required to obtain insurance only on minimum cover. Should the buyer wish to have more insurance protection, it will need either to agree as much expressly with the seller or to make its own extra insurance arrangements."

(Diagram for your ref.)

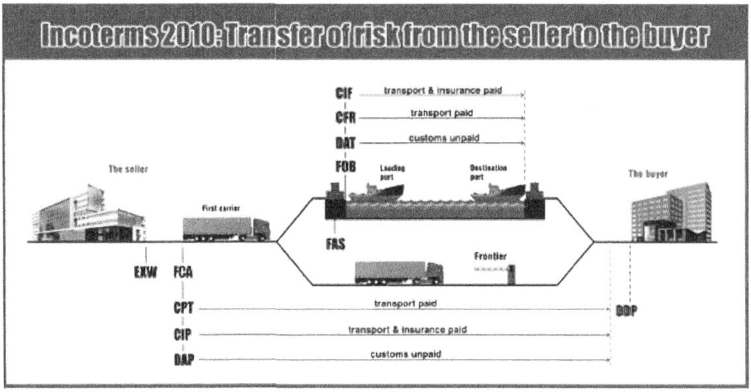

CHAPTER *Nine*

Export Logistic

International Logistics

Export is done through different modes like Air, Sea, Rail, Road or multimode way, etc....

Logistics

Planning, Implementing and controlling the physical and information flows concerned with materials and final goods from the point of origin to the end of usage.

Logistics is the management of stuff, and information regarding the stuff, from one place to another until it reaches the consumer. The logistical management of physical items may include the integration of information (such as inventory databases and shipping schedules), material handling, production, packaging, inventory, transportation, distribution, storage, and security for the resources.

FCL – Full Container Load

A standard (twenty or forty-foot) container that is loaded and unloaded under the risk and account of the shipper or consignee. In general, a full container load attracts lower freight rates than an equivalent weight of loose (break bulk) cargo also called full trailer load (FTL).

LCL - Less than Container Load

This means you share space with others, also share the cost.

If a shipper does not have enough goods to accommodate in a fully loaded container, he arranges with a consolidator to book his cargo.

Shipping Line

A Shipping Line is a company that operates the ships that actually carry the containers (owned or leased) and cargo from load port to discharge port.

A shipping line is a company or organization that owns and operates vessels, responsible for the handling and transporting of cargo aboard their ships. They deal with the cargo from the point of origin to destination (port to port), transiting regular routes on fixed schedules aboard their own vessels.

Some of the Shipping lines like Maersk, Associated Container Lines, CMA CGM

Freight Forwarder

A freight forwarder arranges containers for individuals and companies; they may also be the carrier themselves. They are often the link between shipper and carrier.

Forwarders typically assist shippers across the whole journey to ensure no logistical hiccups occur. They can also provide extra services in the form of advising on packing, completing the necessary paperwork (like bills of lading), providing insurance coverage and custom clearing services.

CHA (Customs House Agent)

Customs house agent (CHA) is licensed to act as an agent for the transaction of any business relating to the entry or departure of conveyances or the import or export of goods at a customs station.

CHA has authorized license to carry out this activity.

Logistics

By Road

Like domestic business shipments are going by road only. The difference is custom clearance activity is not involved in the domestic transport which is involved in the Export and Import business.

By Air

Air shipment is the way of transport of doing Export and Import business.

In this, you need to check the weight and volume of the shipment as freight cost is depend on that.

Packaging should be such to minimize the freight cost and to avoid damage to the cargo.

By Sea

Sea is the cheapest way of transport used in the export and import business.

In sea transport, goods are carried in the containers. The majority of the goods are exported by seaway.

So, you need to study sea transport, containers and How to use containers in the sea shipment.

Containers

A container is any receptacle or enclosure for holding a product used in storage, packaging, and shipping. Things kept inside of a container are protected by being inside of its structure. The term is most frequently applied to devices made from materials that are durable and are usually at least partly rigid.

Each cargo has specific requirements for the containers used for transportation. The several types of containers are specially designed for those requirements.

It is the responsibility of the shipper to ensure, that transportation requirements of your cargo are fulfilled, i.e. to make sure the goods are packed and stowed in the right container and safe conditions, and he must inspect it previously for effect.

Depending on various factors, dimensions and capacity of each container of the same type may be slightly different. The maximum payload of each container furthermore also depends on on-road limitations and/ or on the handling capacity of all ports in all countries crossed between Origin and Destination.

Container Types

These containers are used to transport different types of goods as per convenience and time-saving parameters. For example, Standard dry containers are used to move general dry cargo; temperature-sensitive cargo is moved with refrigerated containers, liquid and powder type goods are moved with tank containers so on...

There are various types of containers –

General Purpose Container (GP) Container

Open Top Container (OT)

The top can be open. This type of container is used when the height of the machines are above the standard dimensions and for top loading.

Reefer Container

The refrigerated container is for cargo that requires temperature control.

Commodities required temperature control like Agriculture commodities, Medicines, meat etc. uses refer container.

Flat Rack Container

The Flat Rack container is for oversized cargo, heavy machinery, construction equipment, or supplies.

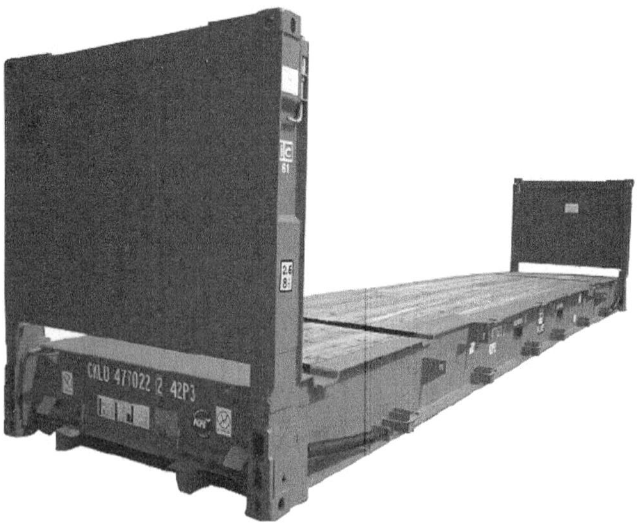

Tank Container

The tank container is for oils and Chemicals.

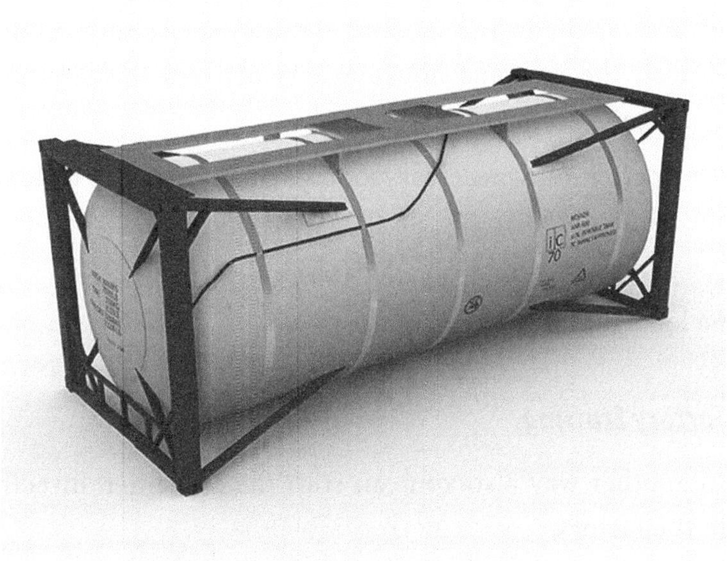

Container Stuffing

Container stuffing means a process in which cargo is loaded into an empty container which is then sealed (often in the presence of customs) and transported to the carrier for loading onboard a ship.

Container stuffing is carried out in 2 ways

Port Stuffing

Goods will be delivered to the port from the factory. Once the cargo unloaded into Container Freight Station for stuffing, the customs house agents file documents with customs to complete customs procedures.

After obtaining LEO - 'let export order' from customs official, as the last procedure of customs clearance under export, the customs house agents delivers the required documents to the carrier.

Carrier files necessary documents with CFS to load the container.

After obtaining the necessary permission, cargo will be loaded into the container.

Factory Stuffing

In another way also you can stuff the container, directly in the factory.

The exporter can obtain the necessary permission to move the empty container from Container Freight Station (CFS) which is a customs bonded area to the exporter's factory. The stuffing of cargo will be undertaken under the local taxation official's supervision, like GST Officers at factory premises.

Once the GST authorities make an examination, customs authorities may not inspect the goods; before giving customs clearance, if they are satisfied that the seals are not broken.

After loading the goods in the container, officers will seal the container.

Many times, factory stuffing of the cargo is used in the loading of Agricultural commodities as there might be damages due to handling of the commodity-like Banana, Grapes, etc.

Factory stuffing is used in the case if you have a cargo loading facility in the factory.

CHAPTER *Ten*

Shipping Documents

Export and Import Documentation

You would have already set up an Export Company by following necessary government rules and regulations.

By choosing your export product, firstly you will find out Buyer or else Buyer will find out to you.

You will send your company and product profile to the buyer and the buyer will send you an enquiry.

After processing that enquiry send quotation to the buyer. While preparing the quotation, take care of INCOTERMS and payment terms and prepare a quote accordingly.

Might be the buyer will ask for samples for checking. After sending the sample, the buyer will test it and proceed further for decision.

After necessary communication and negotiation with your overseas buyer on terms of payment, terms of delivery and other aspects, the buyer will issue Purchase Order.

You will get a purchase order from the importer. Always receive a purchase order on the company letterhead, and it should be stamped and signed by authorized signatory.

The exporter would issue order acceptance or Proforma invoice after thoroughly checking the purchase order.

The terms of payment for your export contract could be any as per the payment terms decided between both of you.

If you would like to arrange finance against export, you can approach your bank for Pre-shipment or Post shipment finance against export orders obtained by you.

If any international quality check agencies like SGS, BVQI, etc. are involved as per the terms and conditions between you and your overseas buyer, such inspection is arranged.

After completing the necessary quality check (QC) formalities, the goods for export are arranged for proper packing to meet export quality.

Palletisation or Crating is arranged for the safety of cargo. You need to decide the mode of transport of shipment by Road or by Sea or by Air. If you are shipping by sea, then select the type of containers and as per the volume, decide whether it is FCL or LCL.

ENQUIRY

The enquiry is sent by Importer to Exporter, asking about the product and other details.

The enquiry should have all details like the goods required, their description, catalogue number or grade, size, weight and the quantity required similarly, the time and method of delivery, method of packing, terms, and conditions in regard to payment should also be indicated.

Detailed enquiry will help to send proper quotation to Importer with all terms and conditions.

QUOTATION

The quotation is prepared based on the detailed enquiry. To prepare a quotation, you need to work out details about the Product, Delivery time, Prices, Payment Terms, and other details, etc.

The quotation is a crucial document, so prepare it carefully.

A quotation describes the product, states a price for it, sets the time of shipment, and specifies the terms of sale and terms of payment. Since the foreign buyer may not be familiar with the product, the description of it in an overseas quotation usually must be more detailed than in an internal quotation. The report should include the following 15 points:

Buyer's name and address.

Buyer's reference number and date of inquiry.

Listing of requested products and brief description.

Price of each item.

Gross and net shipping weight (in metric units where appropriate).

Total cubic volume and dimensions (in metric units where appropriate) packed for export.

Trade discount, if applicable.

Delivery point.

Terms of sale.

Terms of payment.

Insurance and shipping costs.

The validity period for a quotation.

Total charges to be paid by the customer.

Estimated shipping date to factory or port.

Estimated date of shipment arrival.

PURCHASE ORDER

A purchase order is a legal document. That Shows the terms and conditions between Buyer and Seller.

A purchase order (PO) is a commercial document and first official offer issued by a buyer to a seller, indicating types, quantities, and agreed prices for products or services. It is used for the purchasing of products and services from external suppliers.

Purchase orders generally include the name of the company purchasing the goods or services, date, the description and quantity of the goods or services, price, a mailing address, payment information, invoice address, and a purchase order number.

Please Note Purchase order should be on the Letterhead.

ORDER ACCEPTANCE

Acceptance of a purchase order by a seller forms a contract between the buyer and seller, and no contract exists until the purchase order is accepted.

INVOICE AND PACKING LIST

A commercial invoice is a document used for customs declaration that identifies the value and quantity of the shipped products.

What must be included in a Commercial Invoice?

Country of origin/manufacture (where the products were made).

Full name and address of the supplier/manufacturer.

Full name and address of the business or person buying the products (noting if this person or business is different from the importer).

Full name and address of the person or business to whom the goods are being shipped.

Quantity of units for each product.

The unit value for each product (both in US dollars and the supplier's currency).

A complete description of the product.

Port of Loading and Port of Discharge.

Country of Origin and Country of Final Destination.

What is the Packing List?

A packing list is a document used for customs declaration that identifies the quantity, weight, dimensions, and carton count of the shipped products.

The information listed on the Commercial Invoice must match the corresponding fields on the Packing List (e.g., the number of units for each product should be the same on both the Commercial Invoice and the Packing List).

SHIPPING BILL

The shipping bill is the primary document required by customs authority for clearance of goods for shipment.

The shipping bill is an important document required by the customs authorities for allowing shipment.

It is prepared by the Custom/CHA and it contains the name of the vessel, name of the port of discharge, country of final destination, exporter's name and address, details about packages, numbers, quantity and information on each case, FOB price, Total number of boxes with the weight and value and the name and address of the importer.

The shipping bills are of following types:

1. Duty-free shipping bill - no duty or cess applicable.
2. Dutiable shipping bill - goods subject to export duty/cess.
3. Drawback shipping bill.
4. Shipping bill for shipment ex - bond - for goods imported for re-export.

The following documents are required for the processing of the shipping bill:

1. GR forms (in duplicate) for shipment to all the countries.
2. Four copies of the packing list mentioning the contents, quantity, gross and net weight of each package.
3. Four copies of invoices which contains all relevant contents, particulars like the number of packages, quantity, unit price, total FOB or total CIF full value and a full description of goods, etc.
4. Contract no. Letter of credit number, purchase order number of the overseas buyer.
5. Inspection / examination certificate.

BILL OF LADING

Bill of lading (B/L) is a document issued by the shipping company or its agent acknowledging the receipt of goods on board the vessel, and undertaking to deliver the goods in the like order and condition as received, to the consignee or his order, provided the freight & other charges as mentioned have been duly paid.

It is also a document of title to the goods & as such are freely transferable by endorsement & delivery.

B/L serves three main purposes:

- as a document of title to the goods
- as a receipt from the shipping company
- as a contract for the transportation of the goods.

TYPES OF BILL OF LADING

Clean bill of lading - bill of lading acknowledge receipt of goods apparently in good order & condition & without any qualification is a clean bill of lading such bill lading does not contain any negative remark about conditions of goods.

Claused bill of lading - bill of lading with a remark such as "goods insufficiently packed" is known as a claused bill of lading.

Transhipment or through bill of lading - for multi-mode transportation, or when another shipping company's vessel is used, this bill of lading is used.

Stale bill of lading - bill of lading held too long (normally more than 21 days), before negotiation, is termed as a stale bill of lading.

Freight paid the bill of lading - bill of lading issued when freight is paid at the time of shipment is a load paid bill of lading.

Freight collect the bill of lading - bill of lading issued when freight is not paid at the time of shipments and is to be collecting from consignee is a freight collect bill of lading.

Contents of the bill of lading

- Name and logo of the shipping line.
- Name and address of the shipper.
- Name and number of the vessel.
- Name of the port of loading, the port of discharge and place of delivery.
- Marks and container number and container seal number.
- A total number of packages and containers.
- Description of goods, gross weight, volume.
- Amount of freight paid or to be collected.
- Shipping bill number and date.
- Signature and initials of the chief officer.

BILL OF LADING

A bill of lading (sometimes abbreviated as B/L or BOL) is a document issued by a carrier (or their agent) to acknowledge receipt of cargo for shipment.

A bill of Lading must be transferable and serves three main functions:

It is a conclusive receipt, i.e. an acknowledgement that the goods have been loaded and

It contains or reveals the terms of the contract of carriage; and

It serves as a document of title to the products subject to the rule.

Bills of lading are one of three crucial documents used in international trade to ensure that exporters receive payment and importers receive the merchandise.

The other two documents are a policy of insurance and an invoice.

Whereas a bill of lading is negotiable, both a policy and an invoice are assignable.

Bill of Lading is of Two Types

Negotiable and Non-Negotiable

Negotiable means you can exchange the goods against that. The importer can clear the cargo by exchanging the original Bill of Lading.

Negotiable Bill of lading is in 3 originals and on negotiable is like copy Bill of Lading.

Bill of lading is an essential document in Export and Import procedures as without that no one can clear the goods.

As per the rule of RBI in India, documents should be routed through the bank only. So, Exporter should send documents through the bank.

That means all original documents will go through a bank to Importer's bank.

All this procedure will take banking transaction time, i.e. Average 2-4 days, however when the transit time between two countries is very less then might be the problem occurs like Cargo is on hold if its perishable cargo then the goods will be damaged or etc.

In this case, EXPRESS BL is used.

Express BL

An exporter can use this option when you have the time limitations and avoid any further losses or problems.

Express BL means, Original BL will be surrendered to Shipping Line and on that basis shipping line will release Express BL to the Importer.

In the case of Express BL, Exporter will submit Bank set and Customer set to the bank.

Always remember the Bill of Lading will not be regenerated in whatever the case like missing, tare, lost or damaged, etc.

AIRWAY BILL OR AIR CONSIGNMENT NOTE

- The receipt issued by an airline company or its agent for the carriage of goods is called airway bill (AWB) or Air- consignment note.
- It is not a document of title, and it is not issued in a negotiable form.

- The goods are delivered to the consignee mentioned in the AWB, after identifying himself as the party named in the AWB as the consignee/receiver, against payment of charges if any.
- It is therefore desirable to consign the goods in the name of the corresponding foreign bank, as it will enable us to retain the control of the goods, till payment is made/ documents are accepted for payment.

MATE'S RECEIPT

- Mate's receipt is a receipt issued by the commanding officer of the ship when the cargo is loaded on the ship. This receipt is a prima facie evidence that goods are loaded on the vessel.
- Mate's receipt is first handed over to the port trust authorities & on receipt of port dues, the port trust authorities, hand the mate's receipt to the exporter or his agent.
- The mate's receipt has to be handed over shipping company for obtaining the bill of lading.
- The mate's receipt is a transferable document & can be of two types.
    - Clean mate's receipt: this signifies that the goods have been received well in order, properly packed & without any defect or damages
    - Qualified mate's receipt: this signifies goods have not been appropriately packed or received damaged. In this case, the shipping company does not take any responsibility for damage in transit.

Documents for declaration of goods under foreign exchange rules -

- The appropriate declaration forms are:

- GR forms: to be completed in duplicate for all exports (other than by post) including export of software in physical form.
- SDF Form: in duplicate and appended to the shipping bill for exports declared to customs offices notified by the central government which has introduced the EDI system for processing shipping bill.
- PP form: for exports by post
- Softex: to be completed in triplicate for export of software otherwise than in physical form, i.e. Magnetic tapes, disks & paper media.

GR FORM

- GR form is an exchange control document required by RBI. The exporter through the gr form has to assure the RBI that the export proceeds will be realized within 180 days.
- It is submitted in duplicate, to the customs, at the port of shipment along with the shipping bill & the customs certify the value declared by the exporter & also record the assessable value.
- Customs returns one copy to exporter & retains the original for transmission to RBI.
- The exporter is required to negotiate the shipping documents, through his bankers (authorized

dealers), along with the GR form, within 21 days of the shipment.

- The authorized dealer reports to the RBI after negotiation of documents & has to retain the documents till the full export's proceeds have been realized, & after that send the documents to RBI.

ELECTRONIC DATA INTERCHANGE (EDI)

- Electronic data interchange can be used to electronically transmit documents such as purchase orders, invoices, shipping bills, receiving advice and other standard business correspondence.
- Coping with the increasing imports/exports the excise & customs has computerized the manual process of assessment of bills of entry, clearing of shipping bills for export & all documents relating to imports & exports are being processed online.
- At present all types of bills of entry for import of goods under export-related schemes, e.g., 100% EOU, EPCG scheme, EPZ, STP, EHTP, Duty Drawback & Imports for research purposes are being processed on EDI system.
- A new centralized electronic data system will be in place at major ports, airports for speedy and hassle-free clearance of exports and imports as well as to reduce delays in settling duty drawback claims.

SDF FORMS

- On account of the introduction of the EDI system at certain customs offices, where shipping bills are processed electronically, the existing declaration in form GR, is replaced by a declaration in form SDF (Statutory Declaration Form).
- SDF form is to be submitted in duplicate, annexed to the relative shipping bill to the concerned commissioner of customs.
- After verifying & authenticating the declaration, the commissioner hands over to the exporter, exchange control copy of the shipping bill & the SDF form annexed to that.
- This must be submitted to the authorized dealer, within 21 days from the date of export, along with other shipping documents for negotiation.
- The manner of disposal of the shipping bill & the SDF form annexed to that is the same as that of the GR form.

Export of goods & services regulations, 2000. A duplicate copy of Softex along with a copy of the invoice may be retained by authorized dealers.

Documents for the transportation of goods:

- The documents required for the transportation of goods are:
    - Airway bill or air consignment note

- Bill of lading
- Mate receipt
- Combined transport document: ICDs have been set up at various Centres within the country for the convenience of Exporters. The movement of goods from ICDs to the destination is covered by the combined transport document.

Bank Covering Letter

While submitting documents with bank prepare bank covering letter in two copies. And after submission of documents get the signed copy from a bank that they have received the original/other documents.

Submission of documents to a bank

All export trade is routed through the below diagram.

Exporter and Importer finalize the agreement between each other, and after that, Exporter will ship the goods.

After receiving all the shipping documents, the exporter will prepare three sets –

Bank Set – The shipping bill is the document for the bank. So Original and Xerox copy of the shipping bill will be attached to the bank set with the Invoice, Packing List and Bill of Lading.

Customer Set – All original documents will be attached to the customer set. Original Invoice, Packing List, Bill of Lading, Certificate of Origin and all other Originals Documents.

Exporter Set – All Xerox and any other document will be attached to the exporters set.

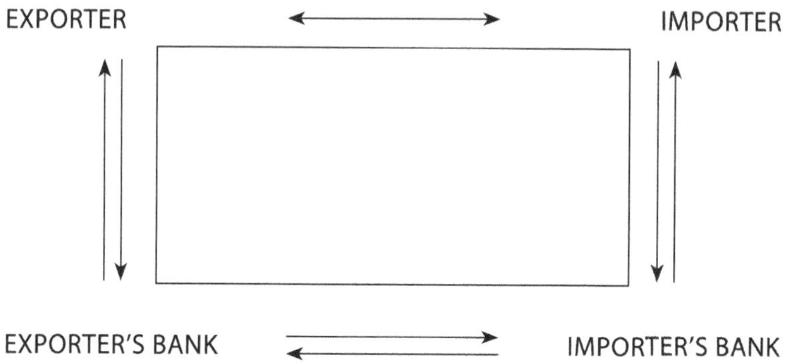

Procedure

The exporter will submit first and second set to Exporter's bank; Exporters bank will submit it to Importer's bank and then Importers bank to Importers.

After receiving documents from Bank Importer will contact their CHA/FF for the clearance of the cargo.

Importer's CHA/FF will co-ordinate with the customs, and after calculation of duties, taxes and all other documentary requirements goods will be cleared and handed over to Importer.

The importer will remit the money as per the payment terms, and the transaction of Export / Import is closed now.

CHAPTER *Eleven*

Payment Terms Modes and Letter of Credit

Many people are curious about Export Import payments. They know about domestic payments but don't know the procedures, rules, and regulations about International Finance and Business.

I just want to say that if you know the domestic business, then you are familiar with the domestic payment terms.

The same payment terms will be used in international business; only the terminology is different.

Domestic businesses are using payment terms like CASH, COD, CREDIT, LC or the Combination.

Let's see payment terms used in the International Business –

PAYMENT TERMS

Payment is a crucial part of the business, and when we say Export / Import, a lot of people stuck in this part.

Many have a doubt about how the International Payment terms are working. Are they different than domestic business?

How will payments be received?

When you learn International Payment terms, you will get a detailed idea about that, and all doubts will be cleared.

Documents Against Payment (D/P) and Documents Against Acceptance (D/A). These represent risk levels lower than an O/A, but greater than an L/C. Both rely on an instrument widely used in international trade called a bill of exchange or draft.

Bill of Exchange/Draft

A bill of exchange, or draft, is a negotiable instrument that is both drawn up by and made payable to the exporter/ seller. Although written by the seller, it has the equivalent effect of a check written by the buyer.

It is generally a three-party instrument consisting of a:

Drawer – the party is issuing the bill of exchange; usually the exporter/seller.

Drawee – the recipient of the bill of exchange for payment or acceptance; usually the buyer.

Payee - the party to whom the bill is payable; usually the seller's bank.

Bills of exchange are either payable at sight (sight drafts) where the bank pays the full amount upon presentation or payable at some future date (time or term drafts).

Here are how they work with Documents Against Payment (D/P) and Documents Against Acceptance (D/A) transactions. (Click to view a PDF process map of the D/A and D/P process.)

D/P – Documents Against Payment

The D/P transaction utilizes a sight draft. Payment is on demand.

After the goods are shipped, the exporter sends the sight draft to the clearing bank, along with documents necessary for the importer/buyer to obtain the goods from customs. The buyer has to settle the payment with the bank before the documents are released and he can take delivery of the goods. If the buyer fails or refuses to pay, the exporter has the right to recover the assets and resell them.

On the surface, D/P transactions seem relatively safe from the seller's perspective. However, in practice, there are risks involved.

The buyer can refuse to honour payment on any grounds.

When the goods are shipped long distances, say from Hong Kong to the United States, it is usually impractical and too expensive for the seller to send them back home. Thus, the seller is forced to sell the goods in the original country of destination at what is usually a heavy discount.

In cases of shipments by air freight, it is possible that the buyer will receive the goods before going to the bank and paying for them.

D/A – Documents against Acceptance

The D/A transaction utilizes a term or time draft. In this case, the documents required to take possession of the goods are released by the clearing bank only after the buyer accepts a time draft drawn upon him. In essence, this is a deferred payment or credit arrangement. The buyer's assent is referred to as a trade acceptance.

D/A terms are usually after sight, for instance "at 90 days sight", or after a specific date, such as "at 150 days bill of lading date."

As with open account terms, there are some inherent risks in selling on D/A:

As with a D/P, the importer can refuse to accept the goods for any reason, even if they are in good condition.

The buyer can default on the payment of trade acceptance. Unless it has been guaranteed by the clearing bank, the seller will need to institute collection procedures and legal action.

Advance Payment

An advance payment, or only an advance, is the part of a contractually due sum that is paid or received in advance for goods or services, while the balance included in the invoice will only follow the delivery.

Documents Against Payments (DP)

An arrangement under which an exporter instructs the presenting bank to hand over shipping and title documents (see the document of title) to the importer only if the importer fully pays the accompanying bill of exchange or draft. Also called cash against documents.

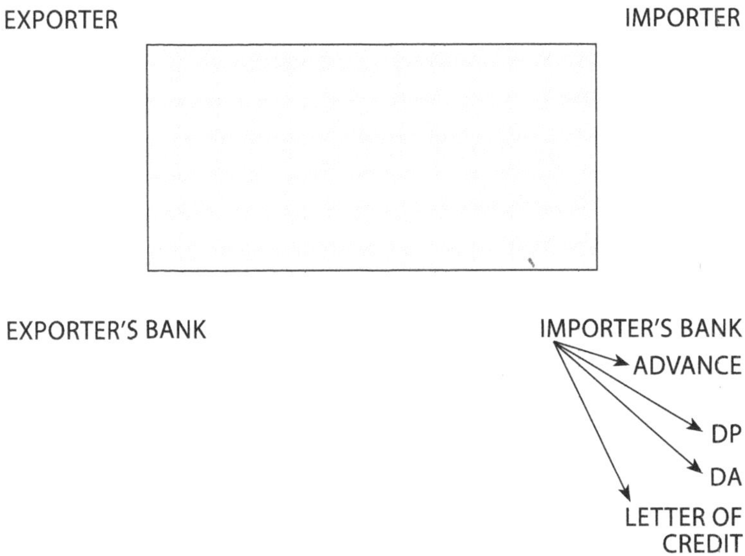

DOCUMENTS AGAINST ACCEPTANCE (D/A)

An arrangement in which an exporter instructs a bank to hand over shipping and title documents (see the document of title) to an importer only if the importer accepts the accompanying bill of exchange or draft by signing it.

The D/A transaction utilizes a term or time draft. In this case, the documents required to take possession of the goods are released by the clearing bank only after the buyer accepts a time draft drawn upon him.

In essence, this is a deferred payment or credit arrangement. The buyer's consent is referred to as a trade acceptance.

D/A terms are usually after sight, for instance "at 90 days sight", or after a specific date, such as "at 150 days bill of lading date."

As with open account terms, there are some inherent risks in selling on D/A:

As with a D/P, the importer can refuse to accept the goods for any reason, even if they are in good condition.

The buyer can default on the payment of trade acceptance. Unless it has been guaranteed by the clearing bank, the seller will need to institute collection procedures and legal action.

Advantages for the Seller in D/P and D/A Transactions

Despite the risks listed above, utilizing D/P and D/A transactions does have a number of advantages for the seller.

The bill of exchange facilitates the granting of trade credit to a buyer.

It can provide the seller access to financing.

The bill of exchange is formal, documentary evidence, acceptable in most courts, confirming that the demand for payment (or acceptance) has been made to the buyer.

LETTER OF CREDIT

A letter of credit is an important payment method in international trade. It is particularly useful where the buyer and seller may not know each other personally and are separated by distance, differing laws in each country, and different trading customs.

It is a primary method in international trade to mitigate the risk a seller of goods takes when providing those goods to a buyer.

It does this by ensuring that the seller is paid for presenting the documents which are specified in the contract for sale between the buyer and the seller.

A letter of credit is a payment method used to discharge the legal obligations for payment from the buyer to the seller, by having a bank pay the seller directly. Thus, the seller relies on the credit risk of the bank, rather than the buyer, to receive payment. The bank will pay the seller the value of the goods when the seller provides negotiable instruments, documents which themselves represent the goods. Upon presentation of the documents, the goods will traditionally be in the control of the issuing bank, which provides the security against the risk that the buyer (who had instructed the bank to pay the seller) will repay the bank for making such a payment.

If the buyer is unable to make a payment on the purchase, the seller may make a demand for payment on the bank. The bank will examine the beneficiary's need and if it complies with the terms of the letter of credit, it will honour the demand. Most letters of credit are governed by rules promulgated by the International Chamber of Commerce known as Uniform Customs and Practice for Documentary Credits.

The current version, UCP 600, became effective July 1, 2007.

Banks will typically require collateral from the purchaser for issuing a letter of credit and will charge a fee which is often a percentage of the amount covered by the letter of credit.

Types

Several categories of LC's exist which seek to operate in different markets and solve various issues. An example of these include:

Revocable/ Irrevocable - Whether an LC is revocable or irrevocable determines whether the buyer and the issuing bank can manipulate the LC or make corrections without informing or getting permissions from the seller.

Irrevocable Letter of Credit cannot be cancelled or modified unless all parties agree

According to UCP 600, all LCs are irrevocable. Any changes (amendment) or cancellation of the LC (except it is expired) is done by the applicant through the issuing bank. It must be authenticated and approved by the beneficiary.

Confirmed/Unconfirmed - An LC is said to be confirmed when a second bank adds its confirmation (or guarantee) to honour a complying presentation at the request or authorization of the issuing bank.

Deferred/Usance - A credit that is not paid/assigned immediately after presentation, but after an indicated period that is accepted by both buyer and seller. Typically, the seller allows the buyer to pay the required money after taking the related goods and selling them.

Additionally, a letter of credit may also have specific terms relating to the payment conditions which relate to the underlying reference documents. Some of these include

At Sight - A credit that the announcer bank immediately pays after inspecting the carriage documents from the seller.

Usance LC - This type of LC offers Credit period e.g. 15 days / 30 days/ 45 days/ 60 days etc.

The importer will pay on the due date of the bill. LC offers a credit period but with a guarantee.

Continuity is the DNA of Mastery.
– KDSushma (Global Fortune)

CHAPTER *Twelve*

International Marketing - How to Find Buyer?

Getting international buyers for an import-export business is one of the biggest challenges many entrepreneurs face. It becomes increasingly more difficult when you're at the start of the venture or are just trying to source international buyers for the first time.

How to Find a Buyer?

Marketing is vital in every business; without marketing, you cannot succeed in your business.

So, tell us, what are the ways to promote your products in Domestic Business List down at least four points –

____

____

____

____

You have listed out the Domestic strategies to promote your product in the domestic market like Advertising, Promotion, branding, newspaper advertisement, TV channels, etc.

There are various ways to promote your product in the domestic market, and people are using ways as per the business.

To proceed further, first need to identify what is the difference between Marketing and Selling.

Marketing

Marketing is the systematic planning, implementation, and control of business activities to bring together buyers and sellers.

Selling

A sale is a transaction between two parties where the buyer receives goods (tangible or intangible) services or assets in exchange for money.

What we have understood from the above definition that Marketing is an activity that generates lead and selling is the part in which actual goods will be delivered to the buyer or customer.

With this view, if we see, we need to generate leads first in order to find a buyer in International Marketing.

We need to strengthen the part of Marketing first and then the selling.

We will see how Marketing will be done

For Marketing, we will check how the Importer/buyer identifies the seller or how he/she will reach to the prospective sellers.

What will be the media to get to know your customers that you are their prospective sellers –

OR How you will create your Marketing presence in the market?

Can you list down the ways –

____

____

____

____

So, we got to know by using the above media we can create our marketing presence in the market.

**Business is changing day by day, so one solution is not applicable every time. Below listed things are defined as per the current market trends in the year 2019.

Website

For every business, it is must to have a Website first.

The website is a collection of related network web resources, such as web pages, multimedia content, which are typically identified with a common domain name, and published on at least one web server. Notable examples are wikipedia.org, google.com, and amazon.com.

A website is an important medium shows information about your business in the form of text or pictures or Video etc. Your customer can get the idea by seeing your website what is your business, what are the products you are dealing with, your positive points, your strength in the market and how to reach up to you.

So, the website is the basic media your customer will reach up to you. In this digital era, we should also go digital so that they can reach up to us.

A first trust will be established when they will find the product or about your company at least the website is there to tell about you and your products.

People will say it's not mandatory, yes, it's not mandatory, but it's an important thing in your business to promote in the Local and International Business.

Please note having a website will not serve your purpose until and unless that Website should be ACTIVE. Learn how to keep your website Active.

Social Media

The definition of business is changing day by day. If we see businesses from the last ten years, people are using traditional methods to do business.

However, in this digitalization world, no one has time to go, meet personally to a customer and to sell your products.

So online things are in demand.

Ask yourself, Are you online, so your customers can reach you?

We have seen the Website is one of the ways to go online, but only that is not sufficient as there are a lot of customers and they all are using various online platforms to search for the product.

To increase your online presence not only in the local market but in the International Market as well, we have to promote our business on the Social Media platform.

Social Media is used to promote the products, Knowledge, business, sharing of ideas and a lot more things.

Social media is the collective of online communications channels dedicated to community-based input, interaction, content-sharing and collaboration, websites and applications.

Different type of Social Media is as below

Facebook

Facebook is a popular social media on which you can create your Profile and Business page.

Create Page on Facebook, share your business profile, photos, videos, information about your business and products.

Also, remember we are not selling anything on the social media, we are just creating business presence over there that means our marketing presence there so people can see you are the solution (Products/ services) for the respective problems.

Create awareness in the market for your product.

Instagram

Instagram (also known as IG or Insta) is a photo and video-sharing social networking service owned by Facebook, Inc.

Prepare your customized posts, Advertises or any short video and post it on Instagram. You can reach the maximum people from the whole world.

So, you are promoting your business globally via this platform.

LinkedIn

Manage your professional identity. Build and engage with your professional network. Access knowledge, insights, and opportunities.

LinkedIn is a professional platform were professionals are connected with each other.

You can promote your business on LinkedIn, about your product, your achievements, your market credentials and a lot about business. This will help people to know about you, your business, and your products, and with this, your marketing presence will be increased.

You can generate lead with the help of LinkedIn as well.

YouTube

Enjoy the videos and music you love, upload original content, and share it all with friends, family, and the world on YouTube.

Though YouTube is used as a Knowledge platform and Entertainment as well, Businesses are using this to promote their business and products.

You can make a video of your product having all the information, a video about your company profile and upload on YouTube.

This is one of the excellent ways to promote your products and business as compared to other visual media; this is free.

Apart from these, there are other social media which is used in the market to promote the business-like Twitter, Quora, Google My Business, etc.

Each social media has different uses; you can choose any one or more according to your Product, Business and Target customers.

Trade Fairs

A trade fair (trade show, trade exhibition, or expo) is an exhibition organized so that companies in a specific industry can showcase and demonstrate their latest products and services, meet with industry partners and customers, study activities of rivals, and examine recent market trends and opportunities. In contrast to consumer fairs, only some trade fairs are open to the public, while others can only be attended by company representatives (members of the trade, e.g. professionals) and members of the press. Therefore, trade shows are classified as either "public" or "trade only".

Trade fairs play important roles in marketing as well as business networking in market sectors that use them. People will seek to meet people and companies at their own level in the supply chain, as well as potential suppliers and potential buyers.

It's good and very important in the business to showcase your products and company via this platform.

With the help of trade fairs, you can build trust and can build your credibility in the market.

There are many governments and privately organized trade fairs in the market, and they are offering local as well as international platforms.

With the good presentation of your company, products and yourself, you can gain the trust of the buyers /customers/importers and grow your business.

Out of all the way out to Find Buyers, Participation in the Trade fairs is a very effective and useful way.

Memberships

We are now studying how we can increase our presence in the local and international markets.

Like by using different ways of Websites, using different types of Social Media, you can promote your business however as said Marketing is the activity where you have to try in every way as don't know which way is useful and effective to promote your business.

1. Register with Export Promotion Councils (EPC):

By registering with Export Promotion Councils, you can stay up to date on the needs of other countries on your product line, what companies are reaching out to them to get information on potential exporters, and how to properly market your business in those countries.

2. Find Local Buyers Who Represent Foreign Companies:

The same applies to every other business. By reaching out to local representatives in your country, you can build an export link to international buyers.

3. Become Active on LinkedIn:

LinkedIn is the foremost global business hub that connects entrepreneurs from all over the world. More global business deals are now concluded daily via interactions that first began on LinkedIn, making the platform highly valuable for global trade.

You can take advantage of this platform by setting up a great profile, engaging with the community, and promoting your services at the same time.

When you build a personal brand people can connect with on LinkedIn with respect to your product and service offerings, people who need what you have to offer will reach out a lot to you.

4. Fill Orders From Local Buyers Who Export To Foreign Organizations:

5. Register On International Trade Platforms:

International trade platforms like Alibaba and several others have made the global import and export business a whole lot easier, as they have opened far more opportunities for businesses who have products and are constantly looking out for importers that can facilitate a certain minimum transaction.

By registering your export business on B2B platforms, your chances of getting international customers looking for businesses like yours to export to them, increases immediately.

6. Have an International SEO-Ready Website:

While registering on an online trading platform, it is highly crucial that you have an international SEO-Ready website. The advantage of this is when international companies or buyers are searching Google for businesses that can export certain products to them; your company would be easier for them to find.

If you use highly experienced SEO experts to scale up your online visibility on search engines, you will not just improve the chances of being found easily online, but also stand a good chance to land on the first page of Google.

8. Hire Overseas Agents on Commission Basis:

You can get reliable sales agents by contacting the Chamber of Commerce, Export Promotion Councils, and independent consultants in whichever country you intend to export products to.

Overseas sales agents will interface directly with the buyers and will always let you know their position on any potential purchase.

9. Contact the Country's Chamber of Commerce:

As stated above, the Chambers of Commerce in several countries can help you not just get sales agents, but can also help you find valuable contacts.

Reaching out to them in a bid to build a supply chain network of international buyers from their countries is a great step to take. After this, you can go ahead to approach the suppliers you learn and introduce your business to them.

10. Participate In Trade Fairs:

Engaging in trade fairs is a great way to introduce your products to international buyers. These international companies usually visit a lot of trade fairs to see what's new in the market, who's selling what, and which businesses are the best options to work with.

China, for instance, is one country where trade fairs are held regularly. People from all over the world travel to

China during their trade fairs, as it is a great time for them to find competent suppliers.

By joining trade fairs in your country, you can advertise your products to the world.

11. Get Import Lists from Foreign Embassies:

Most countries have state-controlled companies that import products in large quantities. You can do thorough research on the countries your products would be a great fit for and contact their embassies in your country, or directly reach out to them through their company's website contact details.

To make it easier, if you can get a foreign representative with connections to help you through the process, getting a signed deal would be a whole lot easier.

12. Internet Marketing:

This involves the use of SEO, email marketing, social media marketing, Pay-Per-Click advertising, and a whole lot more to boost the visibility of your business to prospective international buyers.

This is usually capital intensive and would require you have an experienced digital marketing team to help you create and execute an effective digital strategy.

So, there are various ways of marketing. You have to try most of them, so you can get leads.

Generation of leads is the main part of marketing. After that selling will come in the picture.

Challenge self EVERYDAY.
– KDSushma (Global Fortune)

CHAPTER *Thirteen*

Risk Factors

Risks in the Export and Import Business

Most people feel export business is risky as they got to listen examples of existing exporters who faced the loss and based on that example they made an opinion about the business. Are there risks involved in international trade? If yes, what are they? How many types of risks involved in international trade? How to overcome each risk in import-export trade?

Business always has a risk. Right? It's not only related to International Business; however, when you learn how to handle that risk, then you will be successful in the business.

People will say Export is too risky because when they are thinking about the export market will update them that how anyone incurred a loss in the export business.

And most of the people because of that not taking any initiative to start their export business.

Actually, if we say about the risk, first you need to understand that, Risk is a part of the business.

High Risk = High Rewards

The risk will always be there; you have to learn how to cover or deal with those risks.

We will see what are the risks involved in the export business –

As per your opinion, list down the risks of the Export-Import Business -

____

____

____

There are many risks in the International business, and the main thing is why you feel like this because you don't know what the solution is and you haven't learned that solution which market knows.

Payment Risk - This risk occurs when Importer refuses to pay, or he is making default. It is happening when the export customer/ importer refuses to acknowledge their obligation to pay.

Solution - You can use a Commercial letter of credit as a payment term or get the insurance from the Export Credit Guarantee Corporation (ECGC) firm. ECGC is the Government organization which covers Buyers Risk and Political Risk.

When Importer is refusing to pay or making any default, then as per the ECGC, they will give you Insurance coverage in that case.

Cargo Damage Risk - A cargo may be considered as damaged when it is received by the buyer in a condition worst than it was despatched by the seller.

Solution - Depending on the mode of transport—rail, truck, sea, or air—cargo insurance can provide protection against all risks of physical loss or damage from any external cause during shipping.

There is a different type of Insurance; however, based on the goods, country and other factors, the shipper should decide which type of insurance is applicable to your shipment.

Also, take care of the things what is not covered in that Insurance and check whether it is applicable to your shipment.

Legal Risk - Differences in legal can exist in different countries, which may have an impact on change in Export/ Import procedures, taxation, employment practices, foreign rules and laws, protection of intellectual property, agency/ distributorship and other related subjects.

Solution - Obtaining advice from reputed legal experts and having knowledge of international laws and regulations is advisable.

Also, before starting the export to that country, one should know legal obligations in that country.

Currency Exchange Risk - This risk occurs when you enter into the export contract and when the receivable amount is lower than the amount calculated when entering the export contract.

Might be you will be in loss or in profit. However, whatever the situation you need to take care of this risk

Solution - Through foreign exchange risk management techniques including hedging and buying the foreign currency forward or entering in a futures contract.

Political Risk - Political actions and instability may make it difficult for companies to operate efficiently in these countries.

This implies the threat that some government action could interfere with Export/ Import trade, like loss of property, market share. This is happening in those countries that may have major political instability, which could result in defaults of payments.

Solution - You can connect with the Embassies to get to know the conditions in that particular country; they are helping you in this regard.

ECGC (Export Credit Guarantee Corporation) is a govt. Owned organization helping to cover your Political risk. Ensure to cover your shipment with ECGC to avoid the political risk.

Country Risk - The culture or the instability of a country may create risks that may make it difficult for multinational companies to operate safely, effectively, and efficiently. Some of the country's risks come from the governments' policies, economic conditions, security factors, and political conditions. Solving one of these problems without all of the issues (aggregate) together will not be enough in mitigating the country risk.

Solution - Country profiling is the solution for the same. Study about the targeted Market / Country. The country profile includes the Political situation of the country, Economic condition of the country, Environmental condition of the country, population, gender analysis, etc. study with respect to your business and product. So that Exporter / Importer can avoid the Country risk.

You can connect with the Embassies to get to know the conditions in that particular country; they are helping you in this regard.

Finance Risk - Many of you are thinking that we want to do business but no finance or shortage of funds and a lot of things that is the hindrance to start your Export / Business.

But friends you all know finance can be created, you will get funding from financial institutes, banks or investors, etc.

Solution - For new start-ups, it might be difficult to get funding but remember you need to prove to the bank so that they can trust you. As per the bank they require at least the first shipment you do at your own, and now they can consider your application for the funding.

So, friends, there are multiple risks in the Export business, but always have a mindset you want to get success in the business, you should analyze the risks involved in the transaction and get to know how to cover that risks.

As always remember, Risk is a part of the business that is why business is giving you multiple rewards.

Either you learn yourself or higher someone or get the help of an expert to avoid risky situations. Always there is a solution for every problem; only you need to go ahead. Take Action.

CHAPTER *Fourteen*

Export Benefits

We have seen there are a lot of risks in the business; still, people are starting the businesses; they are dreaming of starting the business and growing it.

Why is it so? Have you thought about that?

Foreign Trade Policy and other schemes provide promotional measures to boost India's exports with the objective to offset infrastructural inefficiencies and associated costs involved to provide exporters with a level playing field. Brief of these measures are as under:

Let us see what are the promotional measures or benefits govt has extended to boost Exports.

Note: These are the benefits as per the FTP 2015-2020 although govt is changing the benefits and promotional measures time to time interval like any increase or decrease of benefit or any new scheme will be launched, or any existing scheme will be withdrawn, etc. So keeping this in mind, one should keep updated self as per the market to get to know the current ongoing benefits applicable to your product or business.

To update self for the International Business (Export/ Import), you can check or visit www.dgft.gov.in

1. EXPORT PROMOTION SCHEMES

Foreign Trade Policy 2015-20 and other schemes provide promotional measures to boost India's exports with the objective to offset infrastructural inefficiencies and associated costs involved to provide exporters with a level playing field. Brief of these measures are as under:

1.1 Exports from India Scheme

i. Merchandise Exports from India Scheme (MEIS)

Under this scheme, exports of notified goods/ products to notified markets as listed in Appendix 3B of Handbook of Procedures, are granted freely transferable duty credit scrips on realized FOB value of exports in free foreign exchange at a specified rate. Such duty credit scrips can be used for payment of basic custom duties for the import of inputs or goods.

Exports of notified goods of FOB value up to Rs 5,00,000 per consignment, through courier or foreign post office using e-commerce, shall be entitled to MEIS benefit. List of the eligible category under MEIS if exported through using the e-commerce platform is available in Appendix 3C.

ii. Service Exports from India Scheme (SEIS)

Service providers of notified services as per Appendix 3D are eligible for freely transferable duty credit scrip @ 5% of net foreign exchange earned.

2. DUTY EXEMPTION & REMISSION SCHEMES

These schemes enable the duty-free import of inputs for export production with the export obligation. This scheme consists of: -

2.1 Advance Authorization Scheme

Under this scheme, duty-free import of inputs is allowed, which are physically incorporated in the export product (after making normal allowance for wastage) with a minimum 15% value addition. Advance Authorization (AA) is issued for inputs in relation to resultant products as per SION or on the basis of self-declaration, as per procedures of FTP. AA usually has a validity period of 12 months for the purpose of making imports and a period of 18 months for the fulfillment of Export Obligation (EO) from the date of issue. AA is issued either to a manufacturer exporter or merchant exporter tied to a supporting manufacturer.

2.2 Advance Authorization for annual requirement

Exporters having past export performance (in at least preceding two financial years) shall be entitled to Advance Authorization for Annual requirement. This shall only be issued for items having SION.

2.3 Duty-Free Import Authorization (DFIA) Scheme

DFIA is issued to allow duty-free import of inputs, with a minimum value addition requirement of 20%. DFIA shall be exempted only from the payment of basic customs duty. DFIA shall be issued on a post export basis for products for which SION has been notified. Separate schemes exist for gems and jewellery sector for which FTP may be referred.

2.4 Duty Drawback of Customs

The scheme is administered by the Department of Revenue. Under these scheme products made out of duty paid inputs are first exported, and thereafter refund of duty is claimed in two ways:

i) All Industry Rates: As per Schedule

ii) Brand Rate: As per application on the basis of data/ documents

2.5 Interest Equalisation Scheme (IES)

The Government announced the Interest Equalisation Scheme @ 3% per annum for Pre and Post Shipment Rupee Export Credit with effect from 1st April, 2015 for 5 years available to all exports under 416 tariff lines [at ITC (HS) code of 4 digit] and exports made by Micro, Small & Medium Enterprises (MSMEs) across all ITC(HS) codes. With effect from November 2, 2018, the rate of Interest Equalisation for MSME has been increased to 5%. The Scheme has also been extended to Merchant Exporters who will now avail the benefit @ 3% for all exports under 416 tariff lines w.e.f. January 2, 2019.

3. EPCG SCHEME

3.1 Zero duty EPCG scheme

Under this scheme, the import of capital goods at zero customs duty is allowed for producing quality goods and services to enhance India's export competitiveness. Import under EPCG shall be subject to an export obligation equivalent to six times of duty saved in six years. The scheme also allows indigenous sourcing of capital goods with 25% less export obligation.

3.2 Post Export EPCG Duty Credit Scrip Scheme

A Post Export EPCG Duty Credit Scrip Scheme shall be available for exporters who intend to import capital goods on full payment of applicable duty in cash.

4. EOU/EHTP/STP & BTP SCHEMES

Units undertaking to export their entire production of goods and services may be set up under this scheme for import/ procurement domestically without payment of duties. For details of the scheme and benefits available therein FTP may be required.

5. OTHER SCHEMES

5.1 Towns of Export Excellence (TEE)

Selected towns producing goods of Rs. 750 crores or more are notified as TEE on the potential for growth in exports and provide financial assistance under MAI Scheme to recognized Associations.

5.2 Market Access Initiative (MAI) Scheme

Under the Scheme, financial assistance is provided for export promotion activities on focus country, focus product basis to EPCs, Industry & Trade Associations, etc. The activities are like market studies/surveys, setting up showroom/warehouse, participation in international trade fairs, publicity campaigns, brand promotion, reimbursement of registration charges for pharmaceuticals, testing charges for engineering products abroad, etc. Details of the Scheme is available at www.commerce.gov.in

5.3 Status Holder Scheme

Upon achieving prescribed export performance, status recognition as one-star Export House, Two Star Export House, three-star export house, four-star export house, and the five-star export house is accorded to the eligible applicants as per their export performance. Such Status Holders are eligible for various non-fiscal privileges as prescribed in the Foreign Trade Policy.

In addition to the above schemes, facilities like 24X7 customs clearance, single window in customs, self-assessment of customs duty, prior filing facility of shipping bills, etc. are available to facilitate exports.

5.4 Gold Card Scheme

The Gold Card Scheme was introduced by the RBI in the year 2004. The Scheme provides for a credit limit for three years, automatic renewal of credit limit, additional 20% limit to meet the sudden need of exports on account of additional orders, priority in PCFC, lower charge schedule and fee structure in respect of services provided by Banks, relaxed norms for security and collateral etc. A Gold Card under the Scheme may be issued to all eligible exporters including those in the small and medium sectors who satisfy the pre-requisite conditions laid by individual Banks.

CHAPTER *Fifteen*

Export Finance

When companies export products or services, long payment terms can often create working capital challenges.

The up-front cost of producing, shipping, and delivering the goods can be tricky for businesses to manage.

Export finance helps businesses release working capital from cross-border or domestic trade transactions that would otherwise be tied up in invoices or purchase orders (for up to 180 days). Export finance is specialist finance that can help a company to grow and increase trade.

There are multiple options to raise finance from various sources like Banks, Financial Institutes, Venture capital, etc.

In Export, banks are providing various options to get finance for exports like –

Pre-Shipment Finance - Pre-shipment credit means any loan or advance granted by a bank to an exporter for financing the purchase, processing, manufacturing, or packing of goods prior to shipment. It is also known as packing credit. As the ultimate payment is made by the importer, his/her creditworthiness is important to the bank.

Banks often insist upon the L/C or a confirmed order before granting export credit. The banks reduce the risk of non-payment by the importer by collateral or supporting guarantee.

Post-Shipment Finance

Post-shipment credit means any loan or advance granted or any other credit provided by a bank to an exporter of goods from the date of extending credit after shipment of goods to the date of realization of export proceeds. It includes any loan or advance granted to an exporter, in consideration of any duty drawback allowed by the government from time to time.

Thus, the post-shipment advance can mainly take the form of:

1. Export bills purchased, discounted, or negotiated
2. Advances against bills for collection
3. Advances against duty drawback receivable from government

You can avail of Export finance in foreign currency or local currency.

Export credit in foreign currency

In order to make credit available to the exporters at internationally competitive rates, banks (authorized dealers) also extend credit in foreign currency' (Exhibit 15.3) at LIBOR (London Interbank Offered Rates)

LIBOR is a daily reference rate based on the interest rates at which banks offer to lend unsecured funds to other banks in the London wholesale (or 'interbank') money market. The rate paid by one bank to another for a deposit is known as London Interbank Bid Rate (LIBID).

So, finance can be availed by way of Pre-Shipment and Post - Shipment way as well.

Government banks and Private organizations are also playing in this field so you can get the loans from them as well.

CHAPTER *Sixteen*

Export Opportunities

Opportunities are not hidden; they are everywhere only you need to search that.

Business is having a wide scope and so

"World is the opportunity" for you just explore it.

Export gives you a lot of benefits as well as the scope to grow globally.

If we compare two persons one only knows about the domestic market and others who know about the domestic and international business/market as well, what you think is the scope and opportunity for both of them.

And I am sure the person who knows export having the highest and better scope than the unknown.

So, after learning the Export and Import (International Business), you can explore yourself in a domestic and global level as well.

Start your own Business –

Do you know business requires investment or not? What's your answer?

Yes, actually business requires investment but let me clear you it is not only the monetary.

To start any business, you need to invest money, time, your efforts and yourself as well.

The good news is without having so much money or no money you can start your export/import/business.

Surprised! But it's true by investing in knowledge also you can start your own business.

By learning about export and import, you can start your own business, domestic or international.

Any small to large level business you can start with this knowledge.

If you are a student you can start working as an agent for documents like you can issue IEC (Import and Export code) and other Export licenses. In this way, you can become the BOSS with low investment.

Manufacturer Exporter

If you are a manufacturer and producing any type of products, but you are limited to the domestic market only then Export is the biggest opportunity for you.

You can export your product directly or indirectly to the International market and earn foreign currency and become a Manufacturer Exporter.

Merchant Exporter

If you are not manufacturing any products or don't want to do that as well but still you are interested in starting your own company, hey it's a good chance for you to become a merchant exporter.

Many people are carrying misunderstandings that only Manufacturer can export the goods or are exporting the goods in the current market.

But Merchant has a huge scope for the export market.

You can procure the goods from the market, directly from the manufacturer or any service provider and by finding the importer start your export business.

Service Exporter

Hey if you are the person who doesn't want to do business in the products or goods then don't worry, you have the scope to export or sell the service.

India is having a lot of scope for the service sector as having many skilled but unemployed population. So, you can use them and create service platforms.

Any service can be exported from India like apart from the BPO, KPO, and software , India is exporting services of Healthcare, Legal, Accounting and Auditing, Hotel and Tourism related, Environmental Services, Entertainment Services, Maritime transport-related, Distribution services, Architectural Services, Educational Services, Advertising services, Consultancy services, Marketing services, printing, and publishing services.

So, there is a scope to be Service Exporter.

Become as a Commission Agent

If you don't have products or services to sell or export, then you can explore yourself as a commission agent, a mediator between buyer and seller and earn a good amount of commission based on the scope of work.

Commission agents also are known as commercial agents. Work as middlemen between Exporters and Importers. These individuals find employment in myriad industries for large and small businesses, depending on their area of specialization.

Commission agents work in countries throughout the world and may seek work from a number of employers simultaneously if their field of specialization provides the opportunity to do so.

These expert purchasers and vendors provide a valuable service to their clients.

Become as a Sourcing Agent

Many people want to explore globally but might be with some limitations they won't.

There are some shortfalls in resources and or skills.

In any of the scenarios or any of the problems if you have will to start your business, no need to wait you can start from any place, any time and where you are now.

A sourcing agent assists a company with the process of locating sources for products and supplies at low prices so the company can save money on production. Sourcing agents may represent a single employer or could run a business that serves a number of companies. The work can require knowledge of multiple languages as well as a good business sense and coordination skills. Pay typically occurs on a commission basis, where the sourcing agent makes a percentage of the order's value.

Domestically, a company can use a sourcing agent to get the best prices. Sourcing agents have connections with domestic companies and know where to find various supplies. They can negotiate with a prospective supplier and may be able to work out discounts and other deals that the company does not have time to negotiate on its own. This can save the company money and may also create a longstanding and valuable contract for the supplier, so both sides have an incentive to work with a sourcing agent.

Companies may also have an interest in an overseas sourcing agent. In this case, they rely on the agent to locate companies they can work with overseas. The sourcing agent's job includes assessing the needs of the company, locating suppliers, and meeting them to see if they will be able to take on the orders. She can inspect factories to confirm that they will be able to meet standards. This can also include evaluations to address ethical concerns like worries about pollution or exploitative labour conditions.

The overseas sourcing agent can also deal with issues like import/export duties, tariffs, and taxes. These can be challenging for companies not familiar with the norms in a given nation to handle. The agent's skills can cut down on expenses and also move goods through shipment more quickly, with less risk of a holdup at some point along the supply chain. In regions where corruption can complicate business negotiations, a local sourcing agent familiar with the community and the traditions can cut through red tape quickly and efficiently.

Consultant

A consultant is a professional who provides expert advice.

They required skills like excellent attention to detail, good organization skills and the ability to work to deadlines.

If you are an expert in the documentation, you can operate as a documentation consultant, good at marketing, then operate as a Marketing consultant, good at Finance then operate as a financial consultant.

So, in short as per the expertise you have and with the knowledge of Export and Import, you can work as a Consultant in the domestic and or International market.

You can start your business journey with no investment.

Freight Forwarder

A freight forwarder, forwarder, or forwarding agent, is a person or company that organizes shipments for individuals or corporations to get goods from the manufacturer or producer to a market, customer or final point of distribution.

International freight forwarders typically handle international shipments and have additional expertise in preparing and processing customs documentation and performing activities pertaining to international shipments.

You can become freight forwarder or logistics partner by working for the company in the goods movement from one place to the destination place.

From the above, we understand there are various opportunities in the market if you know the things of International business (Export and Import).

As said by someone, Knowledge will lead you to the next level, so from Job to the business, from business to the next level of the business. You need to develop yourself every day and learn new things.

Always remember "World is the opportunity" for you all and yes with the knowledge, proper guidance, with timely support you can achieve your dream to be an International Businessman / Global Icon / Exporter and or Importer.

Actually, Business is a Mind game, and One Author Said 80% is Psychology and 20% mechanics.

For doing business, you need to invest and work on your Mindset, your psychology to be successful.

Also, remember Export/Import is a long-term game never play it with a short vision and with short actions.

Believe in yourself, every one of you has that potential, you can create your Global Fortune and start your Export journey. Yes Export/Import is possible.

"You are born to be Successful."

"Dream Big .. Plan It .. Take Action"

Everyone can start their Export Journey, and we will boost India's Exports by creating our Global Fortune.

I wish you all the best for your Fortune Journey.

Connect with KDSushma/ Global Fortune

You can connect with KDSushma and Global Fortune on the following platforms:

Website : www.globalfortunemission.com

Website : www.kdsushma.com

Facebook : www.facebook.com/kdsushma

Twitter : @KDSushma

Linkedin : KDSushma (SushmaKolwankar)

YouTube : KDSushma

Instagram : KDSushma

Email : support@kdsushma.com